THE PURPOSEFUL LEADER

10 Steps to Becoming the Leader You Are Born to Be

CYNTHIA MUSAFILI WRIGHT

The Purposeful Leader

© Cynthia Musafili Wright 2019

The moral rights of Cynthia Musafili Wright to be identified as the author of this work have been asserted in accordance with the Copyright Act 1968.

https://cynthiawright.org/

Editing: Wendy Millgate-Stuart: www.wendyandwords.com

Design and formatting: Achievers World

First published in Australia by Achievers World Publishing.

Perth WA. - www.awph.com.au

Disclaimer

ISBN: 978-0-6486778-8-8 (paperback)

ISBN: 978-0-6486778-9-5 (ebook)

PRAISE FOR CYNTHIA MUSAFILI WRIGHT

HER WORK AND THE PURPOSEFUL LEADER

Nominated for the African Authors Awards 2020 South Africa

I have my copy, and I'm inspired! Thank you for changing people's lives.

—LULU, South Africa

Inspirational presentations.

—LUMKA MANELI, South Africa

Thank you for The Purposeful Leader book. I read it every day with passion. Thanks once again.

—FELISTIUS MUBUKWANU, Zambia

Cynthia Musafili Wright is a phenomenal leader indeed!

—THUTO SETLOGELO, South Africa

Loved and enjoyed Cynthia's energy and wisdom on stage. Great speaker.

—INGUN BOL, Netherlands (Founder FWoC Organisation)

When you get goosebumps over and over again and feel the power of her words. Thank you, Cynthia.

—RUTH SINKELER, Surianne

Powerful lady!

—MELLANY MSENGEZI MARIRI, Zimbabwe

Cynthia, Thank you very much for inspirational thoughts for the day. You were so profound, and I'm so happy to be at the FWoC Global Conference 2019.

—SPAKES CHWAMAKAZI MATWA, FWoC Global Conference

What a beautiful honour it was to meet you. Your fire ignites something in us all. Thank you for sharing so generously and for your commitment to the work.

—ZOYA MABUTO, Mokoditoa, South Africa

Cynthia is the epitome of the power of a purpose driven woman. True beauty.

—MNAHLAPAMK, MMTV

Hi Cynthia, after the talk we had at the FWoC Global Conference in South Africa, I overcame fear. I am starting to do my talks tomorrow at school. Thank you so much for giving me such encouraging and inspiring words.

—Thatohatsi Mofokeng, South Africa

Wow, Cynthia Musafili Wright. Thanks for inspiring me.

—THEKLA MUTERO, Namibia

Cynthia Musafili Wright is passionate about the feminine agenda. Excellent public speaker, knowledgeable about business strategy, she puts purpose to action.

—MASHUDU LEMBEDE, South Africa

Every aspect of you is inspiring and beautiful, your voice, your style and the way you command your space! We are proud to have you!

— MNAHLAPAMK, Female Wave of Change (FWoC) South Africa

The Purposeful Leader *is an inspirational guide to discovering one's purpose, self-belief and achieving success. In this book Cynthia Musafili Wright describes a purposeful leader as an intentional leader with a clear vision and great sense of responsibility. She explains that leadership goes hand in hand with responsibility and action. To be successful one must conduct self-introspection to discover their strengths and talents, move out of their comfort zone and identify a niche to serve. Success has* *been depicted as a journey where one must continuously strive to achieve their goals. Cynthia goes further on to distinguish a leader from a ruler – a leader puts interest of his followers first and leads by example. But a ruler commands what his followers do. She also highlights the importance of positive thinking, determination and courage in achieving success.*

Successful leaders value networking. They connect and surround themselves with people who add value to their lives. They are also open to change and easily change their ideas to keep abreast with the latest trends and developments. Cynthia also talks about mental health awareness and cautions leaders against making unrealistic demands. #leadership #success #responsibility

—RONALD MWAPE, Digital and Sustainable Marketing Expert, United Bank for Africa

To all those who dare to...

Dream it.

Believe it.

Achieve it.

Table of Contents

PRAISE FOR CYNTHIA MUSAFILI WRIGHT V

INTRODUCTION 1

STEP 1 BE DETERMINED AND BELIEVE

Your success is achievable 7

STEP 2 ACCELERATE THE LEADER IN YOU

What sort of leader are you? 19

STEP 3 AWAKEN YOUR FULL POTENTIAL

Finding your life purpose is key 29

STEP 4 BOOST YOUR NETWORK

A key to increase your net wealth 41

STEP 5 COLLABORATION AND PARTNERSHIP

A key to double your income 51

STEP 6 GET OUT OF YOUR COMFORT ZONE

Average has nothing to do with success 61

STEP 7 FREE YOURSELF FROM OLD BELIEFS AND PATTERNS

It's time to become 'unstuck' 71

STEP 8 LEADERS LEAD FROM THE FRONT

...and by example 81

STEP 9 LEADERS ARE READERS

The most productive habit you can have 91

STEP 10 CREATE A HEALTHY MENTAL ENVIRONMENT

A healthy mindset matters 101

CONCLUSION 109

ACKNOWLEDGEMENTS 117

ABOUT CYNTHIA MUSAFILI WRIGHT 119

Introduction

"Our prime purpose in this life is to help others. And if you can't help them, at least don't hurt them."

— Dalai Lama

To the relentless emerging, established and potential leaders around the world. It doesn't matter where you are from, your age, race, gender or position in life, leadership goes beyond a title. Leadership is your ability to take that which has been given to you and move it forward.

Moving something forward means moving it to an expected goal or working under a visionary. Leadership should be quantifiable. You should be able to look at what you are leading and see progress. Now, progress can be defined and explained in so many ways. As a leader, however, if your leadership is not quantifiable, then we employ the question of *purpose*.

What is purpose? Why are you doing what you are doing? Who are you doing it for? How does it make you feel? How does it impact others? How does it make you feel to see this impact?

Part of my leadership journey has involved moving up the ladder in different positions within my career and in society engagement. I had the privilege of leading several teams to expected outcomes and goals, with some successes and some challenges along my journey. Most of the time my leadership was defined by the title I held at that time in my career and life. But there came a point where I did not feel satisfied with my achievements. I wanted more and higher positions to become a better leader. I acknowledged that I was unhappy in my leadership. On reflection, I realised what the problem was: my *why* was missing.

I needed to redefine *why* I was doing what I was doing. I became a better, happy, effective, sought-after leader the day I combined purpose with leadership to become *a purposeful leader*.

The day I discovered my purpose in life, I realised that I didn't need to keep gaining higher positions to become a good leader: I needed to know my purpose in becoming a meaningful happy leader. Leading multiple teams can take a lot of brainpower and time. So it is essential to ensure that you are happy and effective in your leadership.

There is also the aspect of modelling and mentorship that society automatically expects you to perform. Most times when you are leading there are people watching to learn, get inspired and get motivated. And let's face it, others are watching and waiting for you to fail. There is no secret recipe to be a good leader. The tools to harvest and sustain success are the same.

The Purposeful Leader: 10 Steps to Success reveals the tools that I have used and continue to use in my leadership journey and growth for over a decade. These ten steps have helped not only me to achieve success in my life, career and business; they have been applied with success by at least 10k leaders, impacting on 100k others that they are leading and working with. I am confident that you will find these are powerful leadership and self-development tools for your current or next leadership journey.

As you read through each step, you are encouraged to self-reflect via some leading questions at the end of each chapter. These will help you consolidate the knowledge, and perhaps even see where you are already implementing some of the steps and how to improve your application. The first person to quantify your own leadership is yourself through constant self-evaluation and development. The buck stops with you. Implement these steps, find your purpose in all that you are doing, and become the leader your organisation and community need you to be.

It's time to harness the resources and power already around you and within you. It won't always be comfortable, but I can promise you, you can become a leader who leads from the front who others are happy to follow. It's time to impact lives positively. Why else are we here?

Set new goals.

Chances are you have already reached the ones you set last year.

BE DETERMINED AND BELIEVE

Your success is achievable

Good things do not always come easy. Success is built on consistent effort and hard work. It comes to those who diligently conquer all the steps and hurdles they cross on the path to success. Sometimes these hurdles are not external but come from within. This includes the inability to have a stable system in your life, not being able to manage and make the most of the time you have and not having an internal locus of control. Intentionality is key to becoming a successful person, and in turn an effective leader. Only successful people can lead.

Leadership goes hand in hand with responsibility. A lot of people look up to you and rely on you. Hence, being strong headed, goal oriented, focused and intentional is essential to becoming a successful leader that people will follow.

It is crucial to be intentional in all areas of your life. To become an intentional leader, you have to:

- write your goals and take action
- learn to say no
- get out of your comfort zone
- communicate the vision and take responsibility
- give more than your best.

Write your goals and take action

It is important to manage time better as time is money. Once gone it does not come back. Setting actionable goals makes this possible. A good intentional leader sets strategic goals, not only setting them mentally and verbally but also writing them down. Research says that when you write down your goals you are 75% likely to achieve them as opposed to only 40% when you don't. Make sure those goals have actionable steps – and take them.

Learn to say no

We live in a time when people want everything and do not want to miss out on anything in life. So we say yes to everything that comes our way; every new offer, every new project and every new client. When we start saying no to the things that are not relevant, not in line with our dreams and goals and not interesting, we start saying yes to the things that are important and aligned with what we desire to achieve.

Get out of your comfort zone

If you do not push yourself to the limit and stay in your comfort zone, you will miss out on opportunities that can help you to achieve your goals. The focus should be on *acting* rather than *reacting*. A man or woman of words is nothing compared to the man or woman of action. An intentional leader thrives to become a person of action and encourages others to do the same.

Have you ever thought of a professional sailor who, after training, can't set sail because he fears the unknown? He is scared that his ship may capsize, or he is going to be swept away by turbulent storms? That is not a sailor; he's just a fun seeker who remains onshore to catch some fun. Great sailors aren't made onshore. They sail, dare the unknown and break the status quo. Dare to take the audacious move. Don't sit thinking and wishing, and don't be blinded by little success. There is a place called 'more' – a place greater than where you are now. This place only accommodates those with visions and the courage to pursue them. It is the place for champions.

What is your fear? Don't allow the fetters of your fears to keep you at bay, to chain you down and anchor you into believing that you're comfortable. There is no true comfort in mediocrity. There is no true comfort in average. You're a champion. You have no business staying at bay. There is no reward for staying at bay, for being comfortable with mediocrity. There is no reward for being average. Dare to raise the status and create a new quo for the status.

Communicate the vision and take responsibility

An intentional leader does not order his teammates. He builds a relationship of trust so people can listen to him automatically. He does not command but guides and provides a direction to the people, and this is best done by communicating the mission and vision, so everyone operates on the same page. An intentional leader also never blames and takes responsibility for his actions and mistakes if anything goes wrong by him.

Hence, in order to make people follow you and look up to you, you must be keenly intentional and focused — and consistent. This helps to develop trust and credibility, which ultimately results in success.

Leadership is inherent and as a great leader, you'll have to learn to put others first before yourself. A good leader is the first and last in his group. You are the 'servant' of your followers and bound by responsibility to ensure that every member of your team is heard. Their comfort, their ideas and their thoughts should first be considered before yours.

Great leaders are those who put their followers first before considering themselves.

An ineffective leader has no regard for his followers' views and ideas. He casts blames and takes no responsibility for mistakes. He is quick at pointing accusing fingers. Failures do that. Don't make that you. You can effect a great change by deploying humility coupled with vision and belief in your followers. People tend to only follow leaders who are bold enough to not only take them to the promised land but also do so with a sense of maturity and responsibility.

Give more than your best

There is this cold fact that tends to pull us down each time we face adversity. We feel that the end of the road has come and there is no way we are going to push through. But that is wrong. Looking at the successful leaders out there shows something that sets them apart: *They were able to see above their challenges.* They found out that there is always a way despite whatever is going on or coming their way. They knew how to differentiate between what they have to offer and what the requirements of their goals are.

If people achieved their dreams by merely giving their best, then everyone would have been a success. Your best isn't what counts. What counts is what your challenges need to take from you before you can claim you've surmounted them. So, you have to consistently give what is necessary to achieve your goals and not just simply what you have to offer. What you have may not be enough to give you what you need. You must be consistent and tenacious enough to hold on to whatever you're seeking and provide all requirements.

What success demands from us is high, irrespective of what we can simply give. The big question is: Are you willing to hold on even when you've lost all? Are you ready to keep trying when you're down? Are you willing to give your all, your best, your everything and still be willing to give more until you achieve success?

Thomas Edison failed over a thousand times while trying to make the first electric bulb, so they say. But they have also failed to tell you is that Thomas was able to hold on because he realised that he hadn't given his dream all that was required, not merely giving his best. Successful people are assertive people who aggressively pursue their dreams, and the road is never easy. Where we go wrong is trying to just give 'our best'. Realise that success has its own standard, and until you summon the courage to beat that standard you'll always be where you're complaining that things aren't changing.

Why give up? Why look into your dreams and then stray away with the thought that you cannot do it? Once again, I say be strong enough to stay put and consistently give your dream all it requires. That is what sets the divide between an achiever and a non-achiever. Be strong enough to hold on tenaciously and look into your goals. There is always a way into it.

The biggest mistake you can ever make is to believe that you're not good enough, believing that you won't be able to meet the demands of your dreams and your goals. That is a lie. Great achievements were not made by superhumans. They were executed by great minds who only believed that it is possible and knew how to differentiate between their best and what their dreams required.

REFLECTION

Write down your vision and mission as you would explain it to your team to help them get on the same page with you.

_____

_____

_____

_____

What is one of your greatest fears blocking you from achieving your goals?

_____

_____

_____

_____

What are some things you said 'yes' to in the past, which you can now see 'no' would have been a better answer for because they slowed your progress to reaching your goals?

_____

_____

_____

_____

ACTION POINTS

_____

_____

_____

_____

_____

_____

_____

_____

_____

_____

_____

_____

_____

_____

_____

_____

_____

_____

_____

_____

_____

Surround yourself with motivated people. Look after your spirit.

STEP 2

ACCELERATE THE LEADER IN YOU

What sort of leader are you?

When it comes to leadership, one size does not fit everyone. Every person possesses a different leadership style. All you should do is identify that style and embrace it. Even though every person is born with their style of leadership, it is vital to learn particular features of leadership to practice effective management in certain places. Therefore, you must explore yourself and see how you understand situations and approach them. On top of that, when you learn certain styles, you will understand how they can be used to achieve a specific purpose. So, discover your leadership style and accelerate it! In this step, we will be going through various leadership styles so that you can see which one suits you and your goals the best.

Authoritarian leadership

An autocratic type of leadership is ideal for a team seeking strong guidance. It is used in a situation where you must make a few decisions beforehand so that the results are satisfactory. The team, therefore, ends up striving together to achieve a common aim. At the same time, individual efforts play a vital role in achieving their collective goals. You cannot apply this leadership style in instances where your team possesses more knowledge than you do. For example, a restaurant owner hiring a chef cannot teach a chef what to do. So, if your team needs direction, focus and motivation, this leadership style is the way to go!

Democratic leadership

If you are someone who encourages an optimal level of participation from your team members, democratic leadership is perfect for you. You can allow your team members to offer as many ideas and input that they want to make your workplace a better place. As a leader, you collect all ideas and suggestions and decide what the final decision would be. If this approach helps your work to grow, this type of leadership is ideal for you.

Coaching leadership

If you have team members striving to change themselves for the better, this leadership style is effective. You, as the name suggests, are the coach of your team members where you assist them so that they can grow and become a better version of themselves. This leadership style requires you to be motivating, encouraging and have strong control over your emotions since you are dealing with other peoples' emotions more often.

I will just mention here now, too, that it is important to coach yourself too. Most importantly, you should have a strong control over not only your emotions but your actions. Before taking a step ahead, you must think with a strong mind and be certain of all your actions. You must always be able to motivate, assist and work easily with your team members no matter what the situation is.

Lead and never be forgotten

Before choosing a leadership style, you must first objectively view your strengths and weaknesses, the nature of your work, your team members and what your task or goals requires. Then you can choose your leadership style. Once you've done all that, it's important to consider what separates a leader from a ruler.

Nelson Mandela and Martin Luther King were leaders, not rulers. They are so honoured and respected today, not just because they led others or spoke up against evil, but because they put their followers first. A ruler doesn't do that. And then they put their lives on the line to ensure that all their followers were free from oppression. They lived for others and the world rewarded them for that. We are so good at asking the question 'What is in it for me?' each time we are saddled with the responsibility to lead that we forget to ask ourselves what we can do to help others. Martin Luther is credited with the saying:

'Life's most important and urgent question is: what are you doing for others?'

Great and effective leaders carry their followers and not the reverse. They put their all in their task to make sure that the objective of the group is achieved. When you have the opportunity to lead, ask yourself these salient questions:

- How can I contribute?
- How can I make a difference?
- How can I ease their burdens yet achieve the same goal?
- How do I leave a mark?

A good leader leads, but an excellent leader responds and ask themselves the questions above. Think about it. What do you think is impossible for you as a leader? Are there weak people in your group? Encourage them and tell them how strong they can be. Are there people who don't believe in the objective and goals of the group? Look them in the eyes, pat them on their shoulders and whisper into their ears that there is light at the end of the tunnel.

Leave a mark and forever be remembered. Lead like a champion and a general – not a ruler. Don't intimidate your follows; rather, intimidate the goals that you and your team are trying to achieve. Be bold and fearless and be ready to work more than anyone else. Leadership is by example. If you believe so much in it, then do it and make it work. More on what makes a good leader in *Step 8*.

Update yourself

The truth is you are likely to be ridiculed by your team members if you fail to be better than them. Life is all about information, and information comes only by education. Education here does not necessarily mean books. It could be learning to do it better, faster and smarter. As a leader you have to be the last resort for your team members. If they run into problems, they are supposed to fall back on you because they know that as a leader, you ought to have the capacity to get it done.

Responsibility demands that you develop and update yourself to be an invaluable and reliable resource for others. Be an intelligent leader, learn veraciously and scavenge information in a hungry manner. *Step 9* will encourage you to read, read, read.

Be a problem-solving leader and not one that merely gives orders.

REFLECTION

What leadership style have you been operating under to date? How's that going for you and your team? Is it working?

_____

_____

_____

_____

_____

_____

In what ways could you be a better leader to your team? Be specific.

_____

_____

_____

_____

_____

_____

ACTION POINTS

Stop making excuses. Yesterday was the last day of your excuse. Step into your power today.

STEP 3

AWAKEN YOUR FULL POTENTIAL

———————o———————

Finding your life purpose is key

To unleash your full potential and discover your purpose in life, it is vital to reflect on your attitude towards life as well as the number of opportunities you avail yourself of. Your full potential is only unlocked when *you* decide to do so. Once you discover your full potential, success will run towards you. To find your purpose in life, you must follow a few steps that primarily mean having a positive outlook on life. So, empower your mind and achieve self-actualization, which is the desire to become the most you can be.

Think contribution

The late Myles Munroe once said, 'When the purpose of a thing is unknown, abuse is inevitable'. The most important thing in life is to contribute. To give what we have brought and make the world a better place. Ironically, if we fail to think consistently about contribution then we are just existing to make a living instead of making an impact.

I'll tell you over and over that the creator has carefully furnished us with gifts that can contribute meaningfully to mankind. Years back malaria was a killer disease, as was AIDS. The majority of us can remember how the Ebola virus ravaged Africa just a few years back. But since then there have been people who saw opportunities in the diseases challenging mankind. They were bold enough to go back to the drawing board and look for solutions. And today all diseases above are either curable or suppressible to a great extent.

Your potentials have a way of driving you and getting you started. The fact is most people exist to make a living; only a few exist to make an impact. A purposeful like is a life that is driven by energy. An energy that is enough to push you to do what you ought to do. In chemistry there is what is called the internal energy of a reaction. Until this energy is high enough to overcome the activation barrier there will be no reaction.

So it is with your life. You're dormant because you are yet to find your purpose, which means you're yet to find where you belong.

Until a man or woman finds their purpose they are operating from a baser level of life.

Think about what you can give and how you can give it. What difference can you make? It doesn't have to be big and massive. Think contribution! Get a purpose for your life. Seek answers to the unknown and dare to take the bold step that can catapult you to your destination in real life.

Always ask that big question 'Why am I here?'

Think positively

No man can be greater than his mental acumen. He cannot be better than the environment surrounding his mental space. What you think is what you are. Like Henry Ford put it: 'Whether you think you can, or you think you can't, you are right.' Don't be limited by your own mind. Fill it with positivity. You cannot effect change if you are not a positive thinker. You cannot be great at what you have set your heart on to do if you fail to stay positive.

A negative mind is like unfertile ground. No matter how viable the seed you're planting in it, it will definitely die and rot. No negative mind births something great. A negative mind is pessimistic, lacks belief and is always scared of change.

Only you are the master of your thoughts. Your attitude towards life relies solely on the way you think. No matter what your plans are, you should always believe in them. It helps to have a positive outlook towards life when you want to climb the ladder of success. There will be occasional thoughts that you are going to fail along the way. But these are temporary. Don't let them decide your life for you.

Positivity and hope are the keys to attaining your full potential and discovering your purpose in life.

Stop pitying yourself

Everyone faces different problems in life. You are not alone. The only difference between success and failure is found in how you react to your problems. Rather than sticking to the past and pitying yourself for what you have gone through, look ahead and focus on the numerous opportunities being thrown at you. What is life without its ups and downs? Embrace the rollercoaster ride and strive to keep your happiness at the top. Look ahead and don't let your past define your future for you.

Once you accept different opportunities, you will gain exposure and learn so many things about yourself that you initially weren't aware of. Live with the affirmation that life does not have any insurmountable hurdles. Every opportunity is a challenge you must get your hands on.

You are stronger than you think. Step into your power.

You never understand how strong you are until you decide to uptake a challenge. Any opportunity that you embrace helps you to learn something about yourself. The more opportunities you get your hands on, the more you will explore yourself and understand yourself as a person. Once you do that, you'll be able to understand your purpose in this world and live your life optimally.

Avoid being egoistic

Avoiding egotism is as important as avoiding negativity or self-pity. You need to understand that being egoistic will get you nowhere in life. You will introduce yourself to barriers that will restrict you from growing and exploring yourself as a person. Even if you take up an opportunity in life, you might end up learning nothing if you are too conceited or absorbed in yourself. At the heart of contribution is selflessness.

To attain your full potential, you must embrace every challenge that life gives you wholeheartedly. A positive outlook on life will help you understand yourself and assist you in finding your true purpose in life.

REFLECTION

Ask yourself: What is my purpose? Why am I here and what is holding me back from fighting for my purpose?

_____

_____

_____

_____

_____

_____

_____

What strengths and gifts do you bring to the table in your position as a leader?

_____

_____

_____

_____

_____

_____

_____

If you aren't sure of your purpose yet, what can you do to reflect on that more and find it?

_____

_____

_____

_____

_____

_____

_____

ACTION POINTS

_____

_____

_____

_____

_____

_____

_____

_____

_____

_____

_____

_____

_____

_____

_____

_____

_____

_____

_____

_____

_____

_____

If they can't lift you. They can't drop you.
Step into your power.

BOOST YOUR NETWORK

A key to increase your net wealth

We all invest a lot of time, effort and money in our businesses, easily going the extra mile to make sure our business or assets are safe and secure. We make sure that they are protected from every element that could bring about a negative impact or to protect us from loss. But often we do not focus on certain very real assets that cannot be replaced. I guess it is human nature to take for granted things that somewhere in the back of our minds we think are here to stay forever.

What I am talking about here is our relationships, which we often take for granted, choosing instead to run after money and tangible assets. We never even try to imagine what will happen if we lose these relationships. Material things can be replaced somehow, but relationships can't be. It is no doubt very intelligent to make and build money. But it is wiser to build strong relationships.

Social capital is valuable

We often think about maximizing our financial capital and make an extra move to make it more profitable and valuable to our business portfolio. However, many of us can overlook the fact that social capital, that is, our network of relationships, is more valuable and a perfect set of assets for our portfolio. We work with those with whom we share our values, passions and abilities. They know us better, understanding our dreams and goals. This is one of the most safe and secure networks of people around us. And it's because of this network that we can achieve the targets for maximizing our financial capital or profits.

There are different ways to easily build and benefit from your network to make them your net wealth. Your network mainly starts from your own social circle.

Enhance your skills

You enhance or improve your skills from your social circle. It's just like how in olden times people would learn skills from those they spent their entire day with. There are certain skills or smart hacks that you might not learn from your education. Instead you learn these hacks by moving around the experts in some social gatherings and talking about your passion and goals with them.

Meet the experts to achieve goals

There are times in life when striving for your goals when things can be tough. In your social circles you can meet those who have been through your situation in trying to achieve a similar goal. They become your mentors. They already have the right contacts and people for you. They can introduce you to the right experts who can walk with you to achieve your goal.

Fetch those who want to invest

Sometimes we eliminate the importance of having the right people around us. We live our lives as if we can do all that we need to without the help of others. But that is a lie. The importance of the right minds around us cannot be overemphasized. Your companion determines your destination, and the height you can reach is dependent on the people you know. Who you know determines where you can make an impact. It is a basic law.

Who are your friends? What do they think about you? What do they add to you? Do they inspire you to do more or they are constantly telling you to take things easy?

If the people you move around with are not willing to invest in you, to shape you into a better person and create in you that mindset, then you're wasting your time. Investment is simply making commitments today in order to have a better return tomorrow. Find and meet those people who are ready to invest in you and in return you invest in them. They are here to financially build up your goals and help you achieve them.

So if the people currently around you – friends, family or colleagues – cannot pull you out of your current state and push you into another realm where you will be able to do more than you're doing now, then you're in the wrong clique.

Time is the most important asset and it has been distributed among us all equally. We all have 24 hours, and I dare to say that it will be a total waste if you spend yours with people who do not wish you to be better than you currently are. Pull yourself out.

Connect

It is not easy trying to get the connection that can catapult you to your destination, but it is possible. The first step is knowing who you are: someone with a red-hot vision. You may have nothing to show for your vision yet, but you can be bold and audacious enough to step into places. When you have a vision that you're pursuing, a sleeping and waking thought and vision, then it becomes very easy to attract and connect with the right minds. There is something I noticed once when I was young.

In the middle of the night everyone was sleeping but I was awake. There was this dog in the neighbourhood that was barking seriously. I stood up and walked close to the window, wondering why it had barked. I had to go back to bed as I didn't see anything. After trying to force myself back to sleep, at one point something caught my attention. Another dog at the tail end of the street, just metres away, responded. And then another from the street behind ours also responded. Before long the night air was filled with coordinated barking sounds as if the dogs were in the same place and vibrating with the same frequency.

What point am I trying to drive here? The dogs were able to connect. The ones afar weren't the only animals that heard the bark initiated by the dog in my neighbourhood. But they were able to understand and decipher the language of their kind and respond to it. So, who is your kind? What kind of energy do you radiate? What is it that you're pushing out? What is your vision?

Get a life first, have a purpose for your life, and those who can aid you will track down your signal and respond at the appropriate time and in a way beneficial to you both.

REFLECTION

Consider your social network. List all the groups within that network that would contain people who are aligned with your vision and purpose, and who would be willing to invest in you and you in them.

_____

_____

_____

_____

_____

Consider your social network. Who are the people in your life not encouraging you to achieve your vision and don't build you up? Is it time to let them go, or to set boundaries and clearly communicate your vision with them?

_____

_____

_____

_____

_____

What other social networks could you link into to be with like-minded people and experts to add value to your social capital? And don't forget where you also can add to theirs.

_____

_____

_____

_____

_____

ACTION POINTS

_____

_____

_____

_____

_____

_____

_____

_____

_____

_____

_____

_____

_____

_____

_____

_____

_____

_____

_____

_____

Listen to the conversation you are having about yourself in your head. What are you saying about YOU?

COLLABORATION AND PARTNERSHIP

---○---

A key to double your income

In today's era, partnerships and collaboration are essential. Collaboration enables companies to tackle the challenges together and to do so for a common cause. It enables companies to seek support of others when they cannot tackle a problem on their own. It ensures productivity, growth and competitiveness.

Collaboration and partnerships can be formed on any scale. It is not necessary for the companies to be giants in the market to form alliances. Benefits include the following:

- Employees learn diversity and increase their skill set and abilities by learning from each other.
- Collaborating organisations cut costs due to the sharing of resources.

- Improved problem solving through the sharing of knowledge and resources. (Two heads are always better than one when it comes to tackling a problem.)

The power of synergy

If there is a common goal that needs to be achieved, then organisations will unite and give their best shot in achieving that goal. Today's companies believe in synergy. Synergy is a phenomenon that two plus two equals five. The base of this concept is that two companies working together will have a greater performance than an individual company. Collaboration brings a change in the way people think. It enables them to discover their weak points and strengths and all together work for their betterment.

Even on a team level with an individual organisation, collaboration is key to team success. The first question that is asked of a prospective employee appearing for an interview of any giant in the market is, 'Are you a team player?' Being a team player is a crucial trait for today's employee.

It helps in increasing the efficiency because, like I said earlier, two heads are better than one. It enables the organisation to take up on challenges, challenge itself and meet the most impossible deadlines. It increases performance, productivity and efficiency. It enables the organisation to take up a holistic approach. We often see people working in isolation, being busy only doing their specified task. They aren't even aware what steps come before or next. This gravely affects the overall performance of the organisation. You might get the results, but they will always be mediocre.

Working in teams can lift the spirit of the employees if the dynamics are working well. They start liking their job due to the interaction and being able to share their ideas with one another. When an employee feels he or she is being listened to, they automatically feel better about their jobs. This increases retention rates and lowers the turnover rate of an organisation.

Those companies that want to stay at the top of their game are promoting teamwork and are indulging themselves in collaboration and partnerships. This not only helps in creating a better environment but helps the companies to profit effectively and efficiently. So, if you want your company to thrive, prosper and be progressive, start investing in and engaging with your employees to create a dynamic team force.

The Vanderbilt and Rockefeller story

John D Rockefeller is regarded as the all-time richest man in history. He founded Standard Oil and ran it for years until it was broken down into smaller companies by the US government. But looking back to how he started, John D Rockefeller came from a very poor home with an irresponsible father who lived all his life as a con man. John learnt to be independent at a very early age as his father failed in his responsibility and commitment to the family. In his twenties, Rockefeller built his first refinery and was struggling to keep up with production. Meanwhile, Vanderbilt, a railway commodore, was already established and was at the time the wealthiest man in America. He had some bitter competitors and for him to stay in the transport business, he understood he had to outsmart, them.

So he invited the struggling oil man, Rockefeller, over to his house and offered to help him transport his oil to larger markets, charging him a certain amount per barrel. And that was all. It was a win-win partnership, and over the next few years, Rockefeller took over Vanderbilt as the most powerful man in America.

What's your take about partnership?

Do you know that the big brands around us today don't manufacture everything that carries their logos? They outsource some parts of the production process to other companies to save time and focus their energy on something else. Soichiro Honda was known to manufacture piston rings for Toyota before he broke out and built his own automobile company, Honda. Partnership is not friendship. Your interest isn't about what you stand to gain instantly.

Partnership is a long-term commitment to collaborate and build together a working system that can outlive you.

Getting smart

So why sail alone? There are people out there who have money but are looking for the right person with a productive idea. There are companies out there waiting for you to distinguish yourself and tell them what you carry. The key is finding the right people. Look around your production process. What is costing you the most? Can't someone else get it done for less while you use that time for something else?

No big company operates as an island. They collaborate and build ideas among themselves then go to their production rooms and transform their ideas into finished products. Then they unleash the finished products on their customers. What are you unleashing? You have to find the right people and put them on your ship.

You must look for the right people with the right information and then partner with them. In elementary biology we were taught symbiosis. Come on, you didn't just learn that for biology's sake or for passing exams. Practise it. Be a creative mind and hang out with creative ones.

There is no way you can move mountains on your own if you are not willing to pair with other mountain movers.

REFLECTION

Look at your production process. Is there an area that is costing you too much and could be outsourced for less?

_____

_____

_____

_____

_____

_____

List some companies you could outsource some of your processes to, and do some research.

_____

_____

_____

_____

_____

_____

ACTION POINTS

Get out of your comfort zone! Nothing great ever came from that zone.

GET OUT OF YOUR COMFORT ZONE

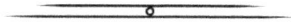

―――――o―――――

Average has nothing to do with success

Your comfort zone is a dangerous place to be as it inhibits your growth and development. People who do not step out of their comfort zones miss out on a plethora of opportunities in life that they later regret when the time has gone. Don't be one of them! Going out of your comfort zone is a key attribute of a successful and prosperous human being.

All the great and successful people in the world took risks and did things no one ever thought of doing, making a lasting impact. That is why Apple brought a change in computer technology and Mark Zuckerberg became a billionaire by creating Facebook.

Sometimes people prefer to stay in their comfort zones and do not take risks, not because they do not want success but because they fear the unknown. Some people believe that staying in their comfort zone is safe as this is where they feel relaxed. But highly successful people disagree and view this as a dangerous place to be in. They know that the more you risk, the more you grow, the more you learn and the greater will be the return.

No matter how talented, hardworking and smart you think you are, if you are not willing to step out of your comfort zone and overcome the fear of the unknown you will not be able to achieve success.

3 keys to overcome fear

To get over the fear of the unknown and get out of your comfort zone you have to: (1) Be clear on what you are trying to overcome; (2) Get used to discomfort; and (3) Treat failure as your teacher.

Be clear on what you are trying to overcome.

The primary emotion to overcome in moving out of your comfort zone is fear. You have to be very specific as to what those fears are if you wish to take that first step to overcome them. Ask yourself what you are afraid of. *Am I scared of introducing myself to people? Is it because I am insecure about my voice? Or because I fear what people might think of me?*

Get used to discomfort.

If you wish to step out of the comfort zone, you should not avoid situations that cause you discomfort. In fact, try to prolong the situation that makes you uncomfortable. Doing this more often will make you used to such situations until they no longer cause any discomfort as they will become familiar.

Treat failure as a teacher.

Many of us are afraid of failure so much that we do not take any risk and prefer to stay in our comfort zones. If we start looking at failure as a teacher, then this paradigm shift will help a lot in taking risks and overcoming our fears. No failure comes without a lesson, and it is important to focus on what you learn as a result of the failure. This helps you to grow and correct your mistakes in the future. Hence, it is crucial to take risks, overcome your fears and step forward to achieve your goals and ambitions because only you can help yourself.

There is no true comfort in the comfort zone

There is nothing as dangerous as partial success. It has a way of taking the biggest chunk of our lives while making us feel that we have arrived. We sometimes condition our minds that there is a destination, an end point, and there is a place where there will be no more challenges. That is a lie. There has never been a war lord who was crowned outside of battle. They make their mark in the battlefield and then get rewarded in the public sphere. To get real comfort you must be willing to sail out of harbour and out into the unknown turbulent sea. That's how sailors are made.

So, to ensure that you remain relevant in the game, there has to be consistent sailing and building of the future. There must be this great shift in your mindset that you didn't come here to be mediocre. Average is good but there is a place called 'excellence'. It is a distinguished space reserved for those who are willing and bold enough to step into the unknown. It is reserved for those who are strong enough to look into the turbulent seas and see treasures in distant lands. And then they set sail regardless of what could happen to them. They carry an optimistic mind that everything is going to be perfect. They prepare for the worse even while expecting the best. Let that be you.

There is no true comfort in mediocrity and that is why a huge percentage of the world's population find themselves in the comfort zone, waiting for miracles to happen.

True comfort lies in taking a bold and commanding step.

It is about looking into the uncomfortable zone, seeing opportunities in it and then daring to experience the discomfort you spot and embracing the opportunities that you see.

Be courageous

Nelson Mandela once said that courage isn't the absence of fear; rather, it is the ability to move on despite those fears. There are millions of people who are waiting at the safe harbour, wasting their time and hoping that one day magic is going to happen. They are currently waiting. How about you? Are you just going to sit there and wait for a perfect moment? Are you just going to come here, wait and then die waiting without the world knowing that you came?

What is keeping you back? Are you currently celebrating little success? Are you okay or scared of venturing into a new endeavour? The world is yours; spread your wings and fly.

Be courageous enough to doggedly pursue your dreams with aggressive pursuits. The world is all yours. Laden your ship with all you need and set sail. There is no comfort in 'comfort' and mediocrity.

Be fearless. Stretch your mind and ditch the comfort.

REFLECTION

Reflect on what is holding you back through fear. What are you afraid of?

_____

_____

_____

_____

_____

_____

_____

What steps can you take to overcome those fears?

_____

_____

_____

_____

_____

_____

_____

ACTION POINTS

What has been said about YOU in the past? If you don't like it, change it. Change your narrative.

FREE YOURSELF FROM OLD BELIEFS AND PATTERNS

It's time to become 'unstuck'

It is easy to get stuck at some point in life in emotions, beliefs and patterns. When you do, you stop yourself from availing of many opportunities that come your way. You may have goals and ambitions, but you do not reach for them because you doubt your worth. Your past experiences make you scared to take a chance. You are afraid to make a decision; it feels hard to move on and self-judgment causes you to lower your expectations. When this happens, you stop growing and feel lack and a constant sense of discomfort. This limits your chances of success.

When people feel stuck, they usually wait for something external to happen to change their situation. But that never happens because the change has to be come from within. Hence, it is crucial to get rid of anything you are holding inside your head that no longer serves you and move on in life.

If you feel stuck in old beliefs, emotions and patterns, you should let go of the past; change your paradigm; and believe in yourself.

Try your best to let go of the past

If your past experiences are preventing you from making decisions and take opportunities now, because they didn't turn out to be good in the past, it's time to let go. Try your best to let go of whatever happened, and with conscious effort believe that things will turn out to be positive. If you keep blaming yourself and do not forgive yourself for things that happened, you will always stay stuck and dwell in the past. The ability to bounce back after every failure is the most important trait of successful leaders. Key to this is self-forgiveness.

Forgiving yourself and learning from your mistakes is vital to becoming unstuck.

Change your paradigm

It's important to make a conscious effort to change your perspective on the beliefs and systems that made you stuck. To best achieve that you can meditate, meet new people, read new book, go to new places and spend time with yourself to listen to your inner voice. Start with making small changes: Everything starts from the first step.

You can start off by making small changes in your routine and your interactions; for example, learn something new, make some new friends, move things in your room. The small changes you make bring a lot of positivity in your life and stimulate mental clarity and creativity.

Seek your purpose in life. If your purpose no longer inspires you to move forward, then you should change your perspective of life by focusing on what makes you genuinely happy and what you are good at.

Changing your purpose will help a lot in letting go of your long-held beliefs and patterns.

Believe in yourself

Trust and believe in yourself! This will help to develop confidence, which will play a great role in getting unstuck. If you are lacking in self-belief, ask trusted friends and colleagues to tell you their view of your strengths. Remember, waiting for an external change is only going to result in lost opportunities. Begin from within by making conscious effort to let go of toxic beliefs and patterns.

Change is the key

The most important thing in life is change, and the most powerful belief you can have is that you do not fear change. Change is the most consistent and powerful force that has the capacity to alter our lives forever.

To take a great leap in life, you must be willing to sometimes drop preconceived ideas and follow what is new. I tell people who are scared of following change to ask themselves what they have been able to do with all the preconceived ideas they are clinging on to. I know a number of large companies that folded because they held on to old ways of doing things. They were stuck in their way of doing things until they realised that the world doesn't revolve around them.

To live life to the fullest and get the best out of it, you must be ready to seek for the newest information in town. Analyse and see if you can innovatively find a better way to get things done. Those who cling to old ways in this modern world hardly make meaningful progress because their minds still resonate in an outdated frequency.

The big question is: *Why do people stick to old beliefs and preconceived ideas?*

They are scared! They don't want to try new ways and products. They don't want to waste time. But a majority are already wasting valuable time and energy trying to hold back and stick to their old form of doing things.

Emancipate yourself and be free. The most successful people on Earth are known to swiftly follow change. They have a way of sensing what the outcome of a hidden opportunity would be, and then they buy into it and make it a revolution. Think about the revolution in the mobile phone industry and in the automobile and aviation industry. All these changes were able to come into reality because there were companies and individuals willing to let go of what they know and try new ideas and innovate.

Let me leave you with a quote from the father of Wilbur and Oliver Wright, the two young brothers who invented the first airplane.

"My sons, if God wanted us to fly, he would have given us wings."

...Today we have the aviation industry!

REFLECTION

What are three keys to letting go of old beliefs, emotions and patterns?

_____

_____

_____

_____

Consider if you have any old beliefs and emotions holding you back that it is time to let go of.

_____

_____

_____

_____

_____

Are there any new patterns or routines you could introduce to your life to make a positive change from old patterning?

_____

_____

_____

_____

_____

ACTION POINTS

At first, they will ask WHY you are doing it.

Later they will ask HOW you did it.

LEADERS LEAD FROM THE FRONT

...and by example

The main difference between a boss/ruler and a leader is that the leader leads by example while the boss just orders his subordinates on what to do. However, this alone does not define leadership. To become a leader, you need to possess certain qualities that other people around you don't.

One of these qualities is to help others grow. A leader will never be jealous of the success of his peers. Instead he will appreciate and congratulate them. This is because a leader can look into the future better than anyone else. A leader knows the impact his support will have on the other person and the project as a whole.

A leader will never think about his/her personal gain. They will always think about the bigger picture. They add value to the individuals and to the entire organisation. Many people believe that it is one of the most important duties of a leader to help others grow. Leaders should always try to spend individual time with their subordinates to help them grow more effectively and more efficiently.

It is a known fact that your business processes are as fast as your slowest link. These slow links that cause hurdles in the business process are known as bottlenecks. It is a leader's duty to make sure that none of his followers or subordinates are acting as bottlenecks in the process towards a better world.

Let's look at some of the qualities of leaders that help them lift others in all walks of life.

A leader listens

Leaders might lead from the front, but they always stop to listen to what other people are saying. Your followers or subordinates might be feeling down due to anxiety or depression. A quick conversation with them can help boost their confidence. You must be a good listener so that the other person feels comfortable and light after sharing with you.

Before you take any action as a leader always ensure that you:

- inform your group members and seek their honest opinion and approval.
- request that while sharing their opinion that they do so without any emotions or sugar coating.
- give them enough room to air their views and opinions without trying to cajole or make them do so out of fear
- ask them what they would have done about it if they were in position of leadership.

Spread positivity

A good leader will always spread positivity. Whether it is politics, sports, business or any other field of life, a leader will always be positive, which is known to have a great effect on the followers. We see many examples of this in sports where the captain or coach gives an optimistic pep talk to increase the morale and confidence of the players. When we talk about the corporate world, a leader will always make his subordinates feel free, creative and comfortable. On the other hand, a boss/ruler will always keep his employees under pressure.

Help others by example

One of the best qualities of a good leader is that they believe in their followers. They know their true potential. They know that the people following them can be as good as them. A leader is never jealous. A good leader prefers people to become like them unlike some so-called leaders who get jealous of other people's success. If anyone is in trouble, the leader will present a solution and then try to implement the solution on his/her own as well. The best way to inspire others is by continuously telling them that their potential is way more than what they expect it to be.

Leadership is a responsibility

The best way to definite true leadership is that it is an avenue to carry the responsibility of others. Great leaders are known to push out and drive the best out of their followers but try also to go beyond this. They are good at doing the jobs of their followers in order to garner their trust and confidence. To be an effective and highly respected leader, you must be the most humble and hard-working person in your team. This goes a long way to making your followers believe in the goals and objectives of the group.

'It takes a whole village to raise a man', so goes an African adage. You cannot be better than the quality of followers you have around you, and your success and failure as a leader is highly dependent on the people you lead. Don't spill vinegar and expect to attract bees. To attract more bees, you spill honey, not vinegar.

Be a leader at the front of everything.

REFLECTION

Reflect on ways you can engage more positively with your team members. Consider team meetings and one-on-one engagement.

_____

_____

_____

_____

_____

_____

_____

ACTION POINTS

Make the most out of your experience.

Explore, inspire and implement.

LEADERS ARE READERS

The most productive habit you can have

There is a famous saying going around like 'every leader is a reader but not every reader is a leader' that emphasises the importance of reading. Reading is the habit of every leader and every person in this world who is successful. Why? Because it is a productive habit that brings many benefits to your personal and professional life: insights, a sense of self, increased creativity and imagination, and of course knowledge, knowledge, knowledge.

Gain insight

Humans are all similar. What sets us apart is our knowledge, and reading is the best way to gain knowledge and insights about any subject. Not only can reading help you gain knowledge of topics you had no idea about before, this is how a human mind grows.

The more information we feed ourselves, the more our brain grows. Reading is a mental exercise.

Sense of self

Reading provides you with a sense of self. It gives you insights and knowledge on what you believe and what you don't. It helps you build a strong personality, which is a trait of a leader. By reading more and more, you are aware of everything that is around you. You start observing more and you start questioning more too. Reading prepares you to bring a change in the world, starting from your own lifestyle. It engenders self-awareness. What you become is what you believe in now. And what you are right now is due to what you believed in in the past. It is all interconnected with reading being the key.

Develops creativity and imagination

Reading helps in developing imagination and being creative in every aspect of life. This is the reason why we make our children read lots and lots of books. It does not matter what genre they read, as long as they have a habit of reading. Once it becomes a habit, it will start to positively affect their thinking and the way they will face challenges in the future. Reading is also a good temporary escape from reality to de-restress.

Fill your brain

When you were born into this world your brain was completely empty and void. You have to learn to recognize the people around you, learn how to speak and do so many other things. You went to school and were tutored on how to do so many things. But even then, your brain can do many more things than you can think of.

There is no way you can effect a change without first envisioning it. It has to begin from your brain. You have to think it and the oils that lubricate your brain while you are thinking is knowledge. Seek for knowledge by reading. Not just reading but reading veraciously so that you can command your space. No man can be greater than his mental acumen. No man can be better than the environment of his brain, and there is no way you can simply get it done without first of all knowing how to do it.

What you are is what you read. Fill your brain with knowledge and arm yourself with it.

A knowledgeable man is a beast in times of challenges and obstacles. He's well equipped with the right knowledge and so doesn't see challenges the way they are as he already has what it takes to conquer it. Knowledge is a tool; it is a key and a solution to so many problems. What do you do with your spare time? A popular and wealthy entrepreneur was asked to list seven things that the rich do and that the poor don't. He started by saying, 'Rich people read books, while poor people watch TV'. It has been so, and it will continue to remain so.

Of course, these days you can also listen to podcasts, and watch Ted Talks and webinars to gain knowledge. But there is something that particularly affects your brain growth when reading.

The ones that command are the ones with the right information — the ones who take their time to read and question the status quo. Read! Learn! Study! Knowledge is power. A man who doesn't read is a dead man. A man who doesn't read is a defeated man who operates from the abyss of life. He is driven and controlled by the man that has the right information at the right time.

Explore and find your niche

Yes, I know the argument; you cannot read everything. I agree but you can't do anything without reading. So as already suggested in this book, first find yourself, explore your soul and ask yourself that deep question that a bulk majority of us fail to ask: *Why am I here?* And then find your niche. Paint out what you want to do with your life then storm the bookshop. Buy related books and read veraciously.

It is your world; it is your life. Explore it and make use of your brain. Step up, and instead of being part of the problem, try as much as possible to be part of the solution. It begins with reading. No matter what you've chosen to do with your life, it begins with reading. I see people who rush to the gym every day just to keep their muscles strong and keep fit. If only they can do so to their brains, the world would be a better place.

Only reading can make you a master of your game.

REFLECTION

Reflect on how you can incorporate more reading time into your life.

_____

_____

_____

_____

_____

_____

_____

ACTION POINTS

Discipline is just choosing between what you want now and what you want most.

CREATE A HEALTHY MENTAL ENVIRONMENT

A healthy mindset matters

Your mental environment is your most powerful and most influential environment. You are only able to read this book and decipher the content because your brain is willing to do so. Everything you do in life is tailored to your brain and what you think, how you think it and when you think it. Your brain is a powerhouse and every activity that is initiated in your body is coordinated by it. The massive machines, powerful computers, heavy aircrafts and magnificent bridges you see are just but a few things that someone's brain has conveniently dragged from the imaginary realm to the physical.

But these inventions didn't sprout from a troubled mind or unhealthy mindset. They came from a calm mind that was able to sit down and philosophise – a healthy mind that was able to connect the dots and make everything that it philosophises about come to reality.

What is stopping you from developing a healthy mindset?

Stop thinking negatively; stop seeing why things will not work out and focus on the things that are possible. Train your mind and your thinking. Program it for success and watch magic happens.

Create a fertile soil

We are creators. The power to do great things has been bestowed upon us. But all that power can be useless if we fail to first create a heathy mental environment where we believe that everything is unarguably possible. Our minds are like a farmland. In order to make the crops that you plant to grow, you have to consistently apply fertilizer. You also have to consistently water it. Same goes for your mind.

A great idea in an unhealthy mind is a huge joke. It will keep hovering in that mind, but there will never be an execution. It will hover for some time, waiting to be fertilized and then die off. Look into your mind and check your mindset. Are you a prisoner of negative thoughts?

Emancipate yourself

You have to be free; you were born to be a solution and a problem solver. You must open up your mind and be able to assimilate the 'manure' and 'fertilizer'. Your seeds need to grow. Start by creating a healthy mindset. Start by making sure that you clear the worries and the doubts out of it first. Then take the right 'medicine'. One such medicine is this book that you're reading right now.

Evaluate how you respond to problems and then make a healthy habit.

Mental health awareness

We all know how health is wealth for us, but we do not realise how important mental health is for our work or career growth. It is therefore the duty of the managers or leaders in the workforce to be aware if employees are struggling mentally or emotionally. The employees and the employers should be able to balance between their personal and work life. This is because that is the only way they will be able to achieve their goals and the company's goals.

There are a lot of companies that do not have an easy and friendly working environment. They place pressure on their employees by imposing heavy workloads. Such companies do not realise enough the worth of their employees who act as real assets in the organisation. Human assets. With proper recognition of their value, and respect, employees often cannot function and perform well because they are not able to balance between their work life and personal life. These employees gradually become a victim of mental health struggles and are not able to achieve goals in life.

Luckily, there are an increasing number of mental health awareness programs and trainings given in responsible organisations to make sure their workers are happy in their personal life and achieve their goals, which in turn enables employee to give their best to the company.

We must make sure to encourage and motivate people in our social and professional circle who are struggling hard to make their career grow.

You should be a maker and not a breaker.

REFLECTION

Consider constructive ways to help maintain a healthy mindset for yourself and your team members.

_____

_____

_____

_____

_____

_____

_____

ACTION POINTS

_____

_____

_____

_____

_____

_____

_____

_____

_____

_____

_____

_____

_____

_____

_____

_____

_____

_____

_____

_____

_____

The distance between your reality and your dream is called ACTION. Take action today.

CONCLUSION

The journey between
your dreams and your destination

Conventional leadership demands that we focus on one thing we are good at and lead with that. I know for a fact that most of you reading this book do not buy conventional leadership, and why should you?

We are living in a global digital village that requires us to keep pace in a disruptive world with so many possibilities in skills transfer, entrepreneurial opportunities and flexibility to run global businesses remotely. If you are like me, you are probably leading more than one or two ventures. Leading with purpose helps us to manage multiple things in our leadership as long as they all align to our purpose.

Finding your purpose and using that in your leadership is the ultimate key to true effective, happy and sustainable leadership. We all want to leave a legacy in life, and sometimes that might be in our leadership and the people we impact along the way, not just in the goals we are reaching for. And I will add, that not all people along the way will join you in your dreams or understand you.

A map shows us where we need to go, from point A to point B. But sometimes what it doesn't do is show us the finer details of how to get to our destination: the weather; traffic delays due to road constructions; unexpected incidents; and the trials and tribulations we may encounter on the journey to our destination.

The question is, what actions can we take between our dreams and our destination?

It was only recently, just on the cusp of publishing this book, that something happened to guide me now to share a little more of my own story. I found tears flowing recently in church when I heard the story of Joseph. His story of betrayal at the hands of his brothers, and his chosen responses to that betrayal, touched me deeply. At first, I didn't know why, until I remembered what had happened to me a few years ago. And now I feel I am ready to share this story. I won't share all the details. They aren't important.

You see, a few years ago, I had a big dream! I had a vision to create an international event that would not only increase the platform and visibility of an organisation I was helping to lead, it would bring many other organisations together, working collaboratively in this vision. To cut a long story short, the event was a massive success and was well received by supporting organisations, businesses and partners.

Then my passion and drive in setting up an independent committee to keep this event sustainable were misinterpreted. My motivations were brought into question, and I was publicly vilified in the most unfair trial court around today — social media. This was a time of deep personal hurt. I felt so misunderstood. I felt I had been crucified in a court where I could offer no defense. All my work to date was discredited.

When my name was shamed on social media by some people in the community I had loved and served with all my heart, I chose to not let it break me. My response was silence. I dug deep. My inner voice said that it was time to have a conversation with myself and to connect in with my purpose in life. Instead of looking up in angry defiance at my accusers, I looked downwards and inwards.

Yes, I was angry. Believe me! In Australian lingo, I was 'gutted'. For a moment I wanted to give up on my dreams. But then I remembered that my duty was not to convince people about my vision, my purpose and my goals in life. **My duty on this earth was, and is, to live a purposeful life.** My vision was too big to die with my title as a leader of this committee or that community. My need to succeed in my greater purpose – which for me personally I feel is guided by my God – became more important than the need to be accepted or endorsed. My faith kept me together.

I chose not to be a victim.

My prayer was:

> *Dear Lord*
>
> *Whatever desolate situation I am in right now, I will rejoice and trust that you have my back. You gave me this vision, the drive and love to serve and be creative. I ask you to give me the tenacity to stay focused and trust the process and journey to my great destination. I will act like it is so and will rejoice!*

My three lessons

It took me a whole year to fully understand what had happened, learn from it and soldier on. The first lesson I learned is that, **in life sometimes, we will encounter challenges and trials**. What is important overall is how we come out of them at the end because there will always be challenges in one form or another. While the injustice I had endured seemed like a social prison situation in the earthly life, it was truly a palatial preparation in the supernatural.

The second lesson I learned was that **not everyone cheering you on is on your side**. Sometimes people will cheer because others shouted, 'It's a goal!' Look carefully and assess who is in your corner. Be wise as to who you tell your dreams to. Chances are you will find people to tear you down. Know who is really in your corner.

The interesting thing is, only a few people rang me to ask me if I was okay. Many just wanted to know what happened. A big difference. And now the very people that shut me out call me today and ask me how I did it! They praise me on the same platform they shamed my name. They call me a great representation of their community, a great model for the young generation in their community.

The third lesson I learned was that **your ingroup can be limiting you**. In my case, this was the community organisation I had been representing. I had to move out of my ingroup and diversify my networks and other communities around me. I had to be intentional about creating success for myself so that I could serve others better in my leadership. I needed diversity to push my vison, purpose and goals further. I went from being local to being global; I took action.

Ask yourself: *Who is my ingroup? Is my ingroup limiting my ability to grow?*

Stepping out of my ingroup has made me so much richer. I now sit in rooms, around the world, with successful and accomplished individuals from various backgrounds. I do not feel intimated because they don't look, sound or dress like me. I know who I am. I know my purpose and I have something of value to say when I am around great leaders. I bring value to every table I am invited to because I know I am living a purposeful life and being there is part of my living that purpose. For me personally, this is intrinsically interwoven with my own faith. You may have your own. Wherever you draw your sense of purpose from, live it. Allow it to strengthen you as you walk to your dreams, and through the challenges on the way.

In the waiting, we need to have faith and be diligent. And not give up on the bigger dream, like Joseph. We need to trust people that have been placed in our lives to help us succeed and grow, because true leaders do that. They help others grow, so they too can be great.

And now when I look down? It's only to admire my steady stilettoes, pointing in the direction of my purpose:

"My purpose in life is to help others by creating purposeful leaders."

I urge you to use your God-given gifts and talents and lead with those towards a purposeful goal that helps others and this world. Where talent lacks but grit exits, we ought to harness our networks and collaborate and partner with others to achieve our goals and lead effectively. Having the wisdom to understand when to increase our capacity when we take on new ventures lies in our ability to understand our capabilities and identify who we can work with to make this a reality.

I am passionate about creating purposeful and happy leaders. I achieve this through my online coaching programs on Purposeful Leadership that run for six weeks, group workshops and one-on-one coaching that only admits ten clients per year. Using my voice to empower people around the world is one of my gifts. I speak globally on Purpose, Leadership and Purposeful Leadership to inspire teams, individuals and organisations focused on sustainable growth in their personal lives, business and organisations. Living in alignment with your purpose, I assure you, will keep your path straight and your heart steady.

I wish you well in finding and claiming your purpose and harnessing it to drive you to be the best purposeful leader you can be.

Let's Connect

If you are interested to my programs, speaking or coaching, please visit:

www.cynthiawright.org.

Let's get connected on LinkedIn and Facebook too!

https://www.linkedin.com/in/cynthia-wright-maicd-7a41a7149/

https://www.facebook.com/Cynthia-Musafili-Wright-164705344275477/

ACKNOWLEDGEMENTS

To my husband Daniel, daughter Zoe, my mum Martha and all my family. Thank you for your love and support in everything that I do.

A special thanks to people that brought my vison to life; Paulo Mukooza (Experienced Executive Visionary), Pamela Grabau (Graphic Designer) and Wendy Millgate-Stuart (Editor).

To my close friends and supporters around the world for always cheering me on and encouraging me to continue creating positive impact in the world.

To the Female Wave of Change organisation for providing the platform for me to launch this book at the 2019 global conference in South Africa in 2019. I love you all.

ABOUT
CYNTHIA MUSAFILI WRIGHT

C ynthia Musafili Wright is a Global Purpose Leader and Speaker, Author, Philanthropist, Social Care Organisational Strategist, Aged Care Consultant and founder of Regions International, a social enterprise focused on capacity building and creating platforms where emerging leaders can grow and share information. Cynthia is the Co-Founder of a global start-up organisation, Building Communities Initiative (BCI), that aims to build self-sustaining affordable housing in Africa. https://www.buildingcommunitiesinitiative.org/

Regions International co-founded with African Professionals of Australia the annual 'Succeeding Beyond Borders International Conference' (Western Australia). http://sbbiconference.com

Cynthia is currently 2019 and 2020 Australia Day Ambassador, Female Wave of Change Australia Ambassador and Australian National Leader for Innovate Africa. https://innovateafrica.org.uk

Cynthia is passionate about creating a positive impact in the world by growing effective leaders. Her success in her career and business comes down to her ability to build and maintain partnerships and collaborations. Her success in life is attributed to the connections she creates with others and the extent to which she can give and receive.

She has created success in her roles as Clinical Consultant in Corporate Australia, with over a decade of senior experience in the social care industry. Other successful roles include: Chief Operating Officer of the *Skilled Migrant Professionals Magazine* with over 13k subscribers; Editor-in-Chief of Australia's very first African fashion magazine *Face of Africa Australia*; and Creative Director in collaboration with numerous well-known names in the Australian fashion and arts industry.

Cynthia is actively involved in the diaspora community. She was the 2017–2018 Chairperson of Zambians Living in Western Australia, leading 4500–5000 people.

Cynthia's leadership is strengthened by her communication and negotiation skills as well as her ability to remain calm under pressure. She manages multiple teams and leads with a focus to motivate and empower by creating more leaders, social changemakers and platforms where people can learn and grow.

In September 2019, Cynthia authored and published *The Purposeful Leader*, which she launched in Johannesburg, South Africa during the xenophobic attacks there. Cynthia believes this book was urgent for South African women in leadership during this time. The book was well received and reviewed by people in top leadership positions.

During the Global Female Wave of Change Conference 2019 in South Africa, Cynthia was honoured to receive, on behalf of Prime Minister of New Zealand Jacinda Arden, the Real Authentic Feminine Leader in a Changing World Award.

Cynthia's passion in social care has seen her develop community engagement welfare programs in Australia and Africa. She is currently the Zambian Aged Care Ambassador and co-founded Building Communities Initiative (BCI), heading a global venture to reduce the current housing deficit of 50+ million in Africa. In introducing BCI to the world, Cynthia made this statement:

"Our purpose in life is to help others. Affordable Housing solutions through innovative design and engineering is vital for global economic growth especially in emerging nations. We cannot limit our ability to create beautiful spaces by using limiting practices. We build self-sustaining communities to help our fellow humans live with pride again." (Cynthia Musafili Wright)

CONTACT:

cmusafili@gmail.com
https://cynthiawright.org